THE MYSTERY OF PROVIDENCE

THE MYSTERY OF PROVIDENCE

John J. Murray

Ettrick Press
98 The Brow, Brighton
BN2 6LN
ettrickpress.co.uk

In loving memory of
Anna Helen Murray
(1968-2019)

A life well lived to the Lord

Contents

Acknowledgements

The material in this book was originally delivered as a set of four talks given at the Annual Family Conference organised by Pilgrim Covenant Church (PCC), Singapore, from 28th November to 1st December 2000. We would like to thank PCC for their invitation to Mr John J Murray as the speaker for this occasion.

Special thanks are due to Miss Nancie Koo, who faithfully transcribed these talks from their original audio. We are indebted to her and Dr Ming Shu Chin for their commitment to making this material available to a wider audience, for the good of souls and the honour of God.

We would also like to thank Mrs Cynthia Murray and Mr Andy Murray for this opportunity to help preserve and share Mr John J Murray's labours.

Introduction

It is a joy and privilege for me to write an introduction to this excellent exposition of the doctrine of God's providence. These soul-stirring chapters were first preached at the conference of a church in Singapore, some twenty years ago. Happily the sermons were transcribed into print and are now here available to a wider audience.

John J Murray was a choice friend and colleague of mine in the Christian ministry. There are vital lessons to be learned from his fine exposition of the doctrine of providence.

We see that God has complete control over all that happens in his universe, even over the very worst of things.

We see that believers in Christ should enjoy full assurance that for them 'all things work together for good.'

We are blessed to see how in providence God prepares all who have faith in Christ for entry into the glorious eternal world of heaven after death.

John J Murray, who here introduces us to such great lessons, has, since preaching these heavenly doctrines, passed away and is now in that blessed world above where God is eternally loved by all his believing people.

Maurice Roberts
Inverness

~ 1 ~

The Wonder of Providence

O the depth of the riches both of the wisdom and knowledge of God! how unsearchable are his judgments, and his ways past finding out! [34]For who hath known the mind of the Lord? or who hath been his counsellor? [35]Or who hath first given to him, and it shall be recompensed unto him again? [36]For of him, and through him, and to him, are all things: to whom be glory for ever. Amen.

Romans 11:33-36

We know that people who are of the world think that everything is being governed by chance. The view is prevalent today that there has been a process of evolution by which the world has come into existence, and that process is still developing and going on. Everything that is happening in this world is happening by chance and by fortune. That is the prevailing view amongst the majority of people in our societies. So many people are governed by lucky omens and charms, by seeking to know the future through fortune tellers and people like that. That is the attitude the world takes up.

But then we think of the attitude even amongst the people of God. Perhaps they do not all have the view of providence that we find in the Scriptures and that we find in the best times of the history of the Christian church. A great theologian in America in the 19th century, A.A. Hodge said:

> There prevails a very unintelligent and really irreligious habit among many Christians for passing unnoticed the evidence of God's presence in the ordinary course of nature, and of recognising it on the occasion of some event especially involving a supposed interest as if it were special and unusual. They will say of some sudden scarcely hoped for deliverance from danger, 'Why, I think I may venture to say it was really providential!' But would it have been any

less providential if they had been destroyed and not delivered. Would it have been any less providential if they had not been in jeopardy at all and needed no deliverance?[1]

That view is held no doubt by many in the professing church throughout the world. Yet it is something that is far removed from the concept of providence that we find in Scripture and that prevailed in the best days of the church.

One of the great blessings of the Protestant Reformation and of the great Puritan era in the British Isles and in other places, was to restore to the church the concept of God. God in his glory, and God in his majesty. Dr James Packer has said, 'Puritanism was at heart a spiritual movement passionately concerned with God and with godliness.'[2] Some of the Puritans wrote books on providence. There are several Puritans who wrote

[1] Hodge, A. A. (1887) *Popular Lectures on Theological Themes*. Presbyterian Board of Publication, Philadelphia: USA. pp.38-39.
[2] Packer, J. I. (1990) *A Quest for Godliness: The Puritan Vision of the Christian Life*. Crossway Books, Wheaton, Illinois: USA. p.28.

THE MYSTERY OF PROVIDENCE

about the thing that we are considering here. One of them was John Flavel. His book has been reprinted as *The Mystery of Providence*. He called it originally *The Divine Conduct*, and he says in the epistle dedicatory to that volume, 'It is the design of this manual to assert the being and efficacy of providence against the atheism of the times, and to display the wisdom and care of providence in all the concerns of that people who are really his.' And if John Flavel felt the need to write that when he was living in the 17th century, how much more we need today to assert the being and efficacy of providence against the atheism of the times.

Now, the word 'providence' is taken from Latin. It is really *video*, 'to see,' and *pro*, 'before.' And it really means *to see beforehand*, or *foresight*, in the sense of taking care of the future, or rather an ordering of things and events after a predetermined and intelligent plan. It presupposes wisdom to devise and power to execute.

The Westminster Shorter Catechism asks the question, 'How does God execute his decrees?' It gives the answer, 'God executes his decrees in the works of creation and providence.' These are the two areas that God is working in. There is a clear distinction between God's activity in creation and God's activity in the preservation and government of that creation. He has made all things, he created all things, but now he is preserving everything and he is governing everything.

It is common in evangelical circles for us to think of a threefold activity of God. He has created all things, he is upholding all things in his providence, and then, in a third area, he is working the work of redemption. Now it is really true to say that there are only two activities of God. There is the activity of creation, which is completed, and everything else is encompassed in the activity of providence. You might say, 'Surely that means that we do not appreciate redemption?' Well, we do appreciate redemption, but redemption is part of the providential outworking of God's decree in the world. Providence covers *all* that God is doing in the world. It *includes* redemption amongst the things that we can ascribe to the providence of God. So God has created all things and now in his providence he is sustaining and upholding all things and accomplishing the purposes that he had from all eternity.

1. The scope and extent of providence

How far does providence extend? Perhaps it would be helpful for us to understand providence in three categories.

a. The individual Christian

We begin first of all with particular providence, the particular work of God embracing every single act of every Christian. The direction and care of our lives, each one of us, if we are Christians, is under the purposeful care of our heavenly Father. There is nothing too small in our lives to escape the attention of our Father. The very hairs of our head are all numbered. That is God's providence in our individual lives.

b. The Christian church

Then the second category is the especial providence of God embracing the whole of the Christian church. What is true of the Christian, what is true of you individually, is true of other Christians. It has been true of other Christians in the past, it is true of other Christians in the present and it is true of other Christians in the future. The church was chosen in Christ before the foundation of the world. The church was predestined to be conformed to the image of God's Son. All that befalls the Christian church in the world is under the sovereign care and providence of God. All things that are happening to the Christian church are happening in order that they may all work together for the good of the Christian church.

c. The created cosmos

The third category is the general providence embracing the whole created universe. Not only are individual Christians the objects of God's providence, not only is the Christian church the object of God's attention, but so is the whole of nature. It is under the providence of God. All those forces and people who are indifferent to God and who are antagonistic to God, even defiant of God, they are all being controlled by that God. Not only is it the individuals in the creation that are being controlled by God but also all the galaxies, all the stars, all the things that make up this whole universe. The hosts of angels and archangels, the evil spirits, Satan himself, are all under the control of God.

d. Three windows and one purpose

These three categories—the personal, the church, the cosmic—are like three different windows providing views of one divine activity. It is one divine activity but we see it as it were in three windows. We see it with the individual Christian, we see it with the church and we see it with the cosmos. God is working out his purposes in all these areas and he has this one purpose.

These three contexts are not insulated from each other. They have what we might call permeable walls. God is working in all these areas, but he is working in them together. Perhaps an illustration will help us. You remember Paul coming back in a ship on his voyage to Italy, in Acts 27. That ship upon which Paul was at that time was under God's providential care. Like every other ship that sailed to Italy, that ship was under the providence of God.

But God's purpose for Paul and his friends who were on that ship was bound up with the life and health of the Christian church. Paul had a mission to accomplish. God was preserving the life of Paul on that voyage because he had a purpose for his church and for his people. And so the redemptive purposes of God are being worked out in that particular case.

But you see, his providential care also extended to all on board. They were all under the providential care of God and yet his purpose for Paul was very different from the other passengers. They came under the providence of God in a general way, but Paul came under the providence of God in a special and particular way. God was guarding and keeping his life, in that journey, in that storm, in order that he would bring him safely to his destination—and he was doing it in order that Paul would continue to be an apostle and minister to the church.

So you have a general providence guarding the ship, you have a special providence extending to Paul's life, and the providence that extends to Paul's life is the providence that has the interests of the

Christian church in view. And so these three areas are all linked up together, and in them all we are seeing the providence of God.

e. One overall purpose

Perhaps the best way to think about it is this. There is one providential order of amazing complexity in which God is working out different purposes for the people within it.

God's grand overall purpose is the manifestation of his own glory. We cannot get away from that. In fact, that is where we must begin. We read in that passage in Romans chapter 11, 'For of him, and through him, and to him, are all things: to whom be glory for ever.'

God's great purpose is the manifestation of his own glory. That is what is motivating his providence— that his name will be glorified. Within that there are subsidiary ends, like the manifestation of his wisdom, his power, his justice, his goodness and his mercy. But God's great motive is his own glory.

Also within that purpose and plan is his purpose to save a people and to make a people for his own possession. God establishes ends and purposes for his people and all these ends and purposes are in order that they might be conformed to the image of his Son. All things are working together for good to those who love God. He has this grand plan and purpose for his church and for his people.

Within that plan there is the life of each individual Christian. That is being guided and directed by God. He cares for each one of them. He loves each one of them. Even in the dark things that happen in their lives—the pain, the loss, the heartache—all these dark providences are being woven together with the good things that are happening to them for their ultimate benefit in time and eternity. For their ultimate blessedness.

So God is working in all these areas. That is the scope and extent of his providence. It applies to each one of us, in everything that happens in our lives. It applies to the church, and all that God is doing to save his church, and to present her as Christ's Bride, without spot and without wrinkle. It also includes all that is taking place in the entire universe. It is all under the control of God.

2. The properties of providence

Let us think secondly of some of the properties or elements in this providence. There are several, and they are outlined for us in the definitions of providence in our catechisms and confessions.

a. Eternal

The first thing we must say about providence is that it is eternal. It is working from eternity to eternity. The Westminster Confession of Faith says:

> God, the great Creator of all things, doth uphold, direct, dispose and govern all creatures, actions, and things, from the greatest even to the least, by his most wise and holy providence, according to his infallible foreknowledge, and the free and immutable counsel of his own will, to the praise of the glory of his wisdom, power, justice, goodness and mercy. (WCF 5.1)

Thomas Boston says, 'God has by an eternal decree, immovable as mountains of brass, appointed the whole of everyone's lot, the crooked paths as well as the straight.'[3] The apostle James in the Council of Jerusalem says, 'Known unto God are all his works from the foundation of the world' (Acts 15:18). God's providence is eternal because he has an eternal decree and an eternal purpose and he is working all things according to that purpose. He knows the end from the beginning.

There is a very sad theology coming into the Christian church, especially in the United States. That theology speaks about the 'openness' of God. Some years ago a man called John Saunders wrote a book entitled, *The God Who Risks: A Theology of Providence*.[4] What he says in that book (and some others have said since), is that God does not have complete foreknowledge of the future. This teaching is becoming quite common. Publishers are publishing these books. Yet it goes away from the Christian consensus that has been held down through the years. Now, when the 'openness of

---

[3] Boston, T. (1863) *The Crook in the Lot*. Porteous and Hislop, Glasgow. p.24.

[4] Saunders, J. (1998) *The God Who Risks: A Theology of Providence*. InterVarsity Press, London.

God' theology says that God doesn't know the future, that is a great dishonour to God. It is also something that strikes at the very heart of the gospel. It is a very serious thing, because our plight as sinners is such that a God who cannot effectively bring to pass his redemptive aims is a God who cannot really help us. If God does not know the future and he does not know the future of the redemption of his people, how can that God help us? It undermines the very essence of the gospel. God knows the end from the beginning. God has purposed the end from the beginning and God is working everything out according to his eternal plan and purpose.

b. Vast

The second thing about providence is that it is vast. God's providence is over *all* creatures. Over our whole constellation; over all the stars. Over the whole of the universe. Over the animals and the birds and the fishes. Over inanimate creation. God's providence extends over everything. Psalm 104 speaks about creation, and says, 'O Lord, how manifold are all thy works! All these creatures wait upon thee to give them their meat in due season.' God's providence covers the whole of the vast universe, the whole of creation in all its vastness.

God's providence also extends over angels and devils, over saints and sinners, over the acts of wicked men and wicked angels. It is one of the mysteries of providence, how God can be controlling the acts of evil men. Our Westminster Confession again is very careful in its wording. It says:

> It [providence] extendeth itself even to the first Fall, and all other sins of angels and men, and that not by a bare permission, but such as hath joined with it a most wise and powerful bounding, and otherwise ordering and governing of them, in a manifold dispensation, to his own holy ends; yet so as the sinfulness thereof proceedeth only from the creature, and not from God; who, being most holy and righteous, neither is nor can be, the author or approver of sin. (WCF 5.4)

God has permitted sin and evil in the world. We cannot understand how sin began. Where did it begin? Did it begin in the heart of an angel in heaven? Is that where sin began? We know where it began here upon earth but also we know that God has permitted sin in the world for the further glory of his name.

c. Holy

Thirdly, this providence is holy. Because God is holy then his providence is holy. He is holy in all his ways and all his works. God cannot be the author of sin. God has permitted sin, God overrules sin, but God can never be the author of sin. James says, 'God cannot be tempted with evil, neither tempteth he any man' (James 1:13). He hates sin with a perfect hatred. His wrath against sin is the holy recoil of his nature against sin. Because sin is the very contradiction of his being, he cannot but hate it. He cannot but reject it. We can say with the Psalmist in Psalm 145, 'The Lord is righteous in all his ways, and holy in all his works.'

The holiness of God extends over the whole of his providence. He does all things in holiness. You might say that the bliss of the eternal world depends on the righteousness and holiness of God, such that angels and saints can have unqualified, absolute confidence in God's holiness.

We read about the seraphim in Isaiah chapter 6. They continually cry out, 'Holy, holy, holy is the Lord God Almighty.' If there was any flaw, the slightest flaw, in God's holiness or his righteousness, they could not sing that song. If there was going to be any flaw in God's dealings with mankind, with the whole of his creation, then the saints could not join in that song. They could not sing that song in the eternity that is to come. The whole basis of their blessedness and their coming to the same mind as God is this, that the Judge of all the earth does right. They know at the end of the day that the Judge of all the earth cannot but do right. Even in the judgment of the wicked it will be a just and righteous judgment.

This is the thing in the providence of God. As one man has said, 'The plan of providence is such that sin will be stigmatised and sinners punished, where holiness will be honoured and those who are holy rewarded.'[5] There is going to be a judgment, at the end of the day, and it is going to be a holy judgment.

---

[5] Woods, Leonard. (1851) *Works*. John P. Jewett and Company, Boston: USA. Vol 2, p.11.

Everyone is going to see that it is a holy judgment. There will be no doubt about it. The providence of God will bring it about. 'Great and marvellous are thy works,' is the song of Moses and the Lamb. 'Great and marvellous are thy works, Lord God Almighty; just and true are thy ways, thou King of saints' (Revelation 15:3). That is going to be the song of the new heavens and the new earth. The righteous are going to join in that song and are going to proclaim God as the one who is just and right in all his ways.

d. Wise

Then fourthly, the providence of God is wise. Now wisdom presupposes knowledge. It is one thing to have knowledge, it is another thing to have wisdom. You see, God knows all things. In his infinite knowledge he has this comprehensive intuition. God knows all things. But that knowledge of God is put into practice in the wisdom of God. He does it in the election of ends, general and special. The first end he has is to glorify his own name. The great end that he is working to is his own glory. The other end that is being worked out is the salvation of his people. Everything that is taking place in the universe is directed to the glory of God and to the salvation of his people.

Now what shows his wisdom is this: that he has selected the best means to bring about these ends. That is how the wisdom of God is displayed. It is certainly displayed in creation, but it is displayed most wonderfully in providence as he brings about these high and glorious ends.

One way in particular in which his wisdom is displayed is in the choice of the way of salvation through a crucified Redeemer. What a marvellous display of the wisdom of God in providence is seen in that he has chosen this way of saving sinners— through the death of his own Son! It is a way that brings glory to him. It is a way that honours all his attributes—his justice, his holiness, his love and his mercy—and at the same time saves sinners. And not only saves them in justification but saves them in sanctification. The people he puts right with himself he makes right as well.

The wisdom that is displayed in his providence and all the outworking of it you can see right through the whole history of redemption. God's way of bringing about these ends is marvellous.

e. Powerful

The providence of God is not only eternal, it is not only vast, it is not only holy, it is not only wise, but also it is powerful.

God's providence not only concerns us, it also *executes*. It has power to work. We may consult and we may have plans, but we cannot independently bring our plans into execution. But providence can put plans into execution. It is powerful. It not only devises but it also puts into operation. It not only sees how evil may be prevented but it actually prevents evil.

It is so powerful, this providence, that it brings good out of evil. That is a marvellous thing—that there is evil in the world through the fallen angels and through fallen men and through Satan, but God brings good out of evil. That is the amazing thing— that bad angels and bad men serve God's designs while they intend no such thing. They do not want to serve God's ends. Satan wants to crucify the Lord of glory and when Jesus dies on the cross he thinks he has accomplished something wonderful. But what has he done? He has accomplished God's ends. He did not want to, he did not intend to, but that is the marvellous power of providence. God does it. He brings good out of evil.

God is also able to give efficiency to the most contemptible things in the world. Things that are despised by the world, like the cross of the Lord Jesus Christ—to the Greeks it is foolishness, to the Jews a stumbling block—but, you see, it is the power and wisdom of God. God's providence gives great efficacy to that which in the eyes of the world is most contemptible.

This powerful providence also secures the accomplishment of the very best ends. At the end of the day God's great end will be accomplished.

3. Encouragements from providence

So we have the scope and extent of providence. And we have the properties of providence. I just want to draw some conclusions from these things that we have been talking about.

a. God reigns

The first thing that should encourage us as we view the providence of God is that God reigns and God rules. As William S. Plumer says,

> To deny God's providence is as atheistical as to deny his existence ... Nothing more derogatory to the character of God can possibly be said, than that he does not rule the world.[6]

There are some people who believe in the existence of God and who believe many things about God, but do not go as far as to say that God rules the

---

[6] Plumer, W.S. (1993) *Jehovah-Jireh: A Treatise on Providence*. Sprinkle Publications, Harrisonburg: USA. p.10-11. Mr Murray commented at the time of delivering these addresses, 'There is a book called *Jehovah Jireh: A Treatise on Providence* by William Plumer. I just discovered this a few weeks ago and I have been greatly indebted to him for this work for the material I have been using.'

world. But what we have seen about this providence tells us that God rules the world.

Plumer continues,

> A God, who neither sees, nor hears, nor knows, nor cares, nor helps, nor saves, is a vanity, and can never claim homage from intelligent men. Such a god should be derided, not worshipped. ...
>
> The world may as well be without a God, as have one who is incompetent to rule it, or, who, wrapping himself in a mantle of infinite indifference, abandons creation to the governance of puny mortals, to the rule of devils, or to the sway of a blind fortuity.[7]

If we are going to say that God does not rule the world, if he is not a sovereign God, he is not a God who is worthy to be worshipped. If there is any way in which God is not in control then we cannot adore him and worship him as we do. To surrender in whole or part his control of the universe would be to admit that he was not God and another was as strong as he. If God is not ruling the universe—

---

[7] *Op. cit.*

indeed if God does not hold the hearts of the wicked in his hands and entirely control them—how can the pious pray for deliverance from wicked men with any hope that they will be heard and answered? If God should resign his control over everything even for an hour, no mortal can trace the consequences of that. God's providence is over all the actions of all creatures. If anyone could act independently, that creature would be a god. 'If Jehovah governs not a man for a day, that day he is a god,'[8] as Plumer puts it. Independence is one of the essential attributes of Jehovah. To put a single act of any creature beyond divine control would be admission that besides the Most High there is some other god. If wicked men can act independently without the overruling of God's providence then this is not the God of Scripture. That is the first thing that we must remember.

b. God reigns personally

Then a second thing we must remember for our encouragement is that the God who rules is a

---

[8] *Ibid.* p.26.

person—our heavenly Father. People think that if
you believe in predestination, then you believe in
fatalism. That is the conclusion that many people
come to. In fact there was a group of Presbyterians
in the United States about 200 years ago, the
Cumberland Presbyterian Church, and they came
to the belief that what was taught in the
Westminster Confession of Faith about
predestination amounted to fatalism. They had this
problem. Dr B.B. Warfield speaks about them like
this.

> Is it not remarkable that men with hearts on fire
> with love to God should not know him from Fate?
> Of course, the reason is not far to seek. Like other
> men, ... they have a natural objection to being
> 'controlled.' They wish to be the architects of their
> own fortunes, the determiners of their own
> destinies; though why they should fancy they
> could do that better for themselves than God can
> be trusted to do it for them, it puzzles one to
> understand.[9]

[9] Warfield, B.B. (2005) 'What fatalism is.' In: *Selected Shorter Writings*. P&R Publishing, Philippsburg: USA. Vol. 1, pp.393-394.

And this is the problem, that people tend to identify predestination with fatalism. Warfield goes on to say, 'there is therefore no heresy so great, no heresy that so utterly tears religion up by the roots, as the heresy that thinks of God under the analogy of natural force and forgets that he is a person.'[10]

Yes, there is predestination. God has planned and purposed everything that comes to pass. But it is not a blind force that is governing the universe. It is a person, God the Father. B.B. Warfield uses this very touching illustration about a little Dutch boy.

> This little boy's home was on a dyke in Holland, near a great windmill, whose long arms swept so close to the ground as to endanger those who carelessly strayed under them. But he was very fond of playing precisely under this mill. His anxious parents had forbidden him to go near it; and, when his stubborn will did not give way, had sought to frighten him away from it by arousing his imagination to the terror of being struck by the arms and carried up into the air to have life beaten out of him by their ceaseless strokes. One day, heedless of their warning, he strayed again under

---

[10] *Ibid*, p.395.

the dangerous arms, and was soon absorbed in his play there—forgetful of everything but his present pleasures. Perhaps, he was half conscious of a breeze springing up; and somewhere in the depth of his soul, he may have been obscurely aware of the danger with which he had been threatened. At any rate, suddenly, as he played, he was violently smitten from behind, and found himself swung all at once, with his head downward, up into the air; and then the blows came, swift and hard! O what a sinking of the heart! O what a horror of great darkness! It had come then! And he was gone! In his terrified writhing, he twisted himself about, and looking up, saw not the immeasurable expanse of the heavens above him but his father's face. At once, he realised, with a great revulsion, that he was not caught in the mill, but was only receiving the threatened punishment of his disobedience. He melted into tears, not of pain, but of relief and joy. In that moment, he understood the difference between falling into the grinding power of a machine and into the loving hands of a father.[11]

---

[11] *Ibid*, pp.395-396.

That is the one who is in control of the universe. And that is the one who is in control of the church, and the one who is in control of our lives. It is our Father in heaven.

c. God reigns in Christ

The God who rules in providence is the God who does so in the person of his own Son. He is not only a person who is in control of the universe and directing all things for his glory and his church's good, but you see, the reins of government are in the hand of his Son, the Lord Jesus Christ.

Now we sometimes make the mistake (as I said earlier) of making too sharp a distinction between providence and grace. Again B.B. Warfield is very helpful in this. So many people look upon a severe God of providence and a good God of grace. Warfield says there is however but one God and he is the God both of providence and grace. The two can never be separated, nor can one suffer for lack of support from the other. The two areas are working together. He is the God of providence and the God of grace.

What has this God of providence done? He tells us in Ephesians 1. Paul says that the power that is working in us 'is the power that was wrought in Christ when God raised him from the dead and set him at his own right hand, far above all principality and power, … and hath put all things under his feet, and gave him to be head over all things to the church.' All things are under his feet and he has given him to be head over all things to his church. This is the one who is in control of the providence of God. It is in the hands of Christ, the Son of God.

It is interesting to think of the 'all things' of Scripture. We mentioned one of them at the beginning: 'of him and through him and to him are all things' (Romans 11:36). The whole providence is working to the glory of God. But now we are told that 'all things,' everything in the universe, are under the feet of Christ. Nothing is excluded. Here is the one who is controlling the providence of God. It is in the hands of our Redeemer. Everything is in his hands to bring about his purposes for his church and for every individual believer, every Christian.

Then you go to Romans chapter 8 and what do you find in verse 28? 'All things work together for good to them that love God.' Nothing is excluded. All things are for the glory of God. All things are under the feet of Christ. All things are working together.

And there is one more thing. Paul says towards the end of Romans 8, 'In all these things we are more than conquerors through him that loved us.' Yes, some of these Christians were being slain, and being thrown to the lions. They were being persecuted, they were going through horrendous suffering and difficulties. Yet, Paul says, 'in all these things,' nothing excluded, we are more than conquerors through Christ. You can think of the worst fate that is coming to a Christian. How many Christians tonight are suffering throughout this world, going through tremendous sufferings! But you see, in the providence of God, in all these things they are more than conquerors through him that loved them.

That is the providence of God. It covers everything. I will conclude with the words of B.B. Warfield (I have depended quite a lot on him, he is so excellent these areas). This is what he says, and it sums up everything.

> A firm faith in the universal providence of God is the solution of all earthly troubles. It is almost equally true that a clear and full apprehension of the universal providence of God is the solution of most theological problems. Most of the religious difficulties with which men disturb their minds, rest on the subtle intrusion into our thinking of what we may call 'deistic postulates,' and would vanish could but the full meaning of God's universal providence enter and condition all our thinking. It is because we forget this great truth that we vex and puzzle ourselves over difficulties which seem to be insoluble, but which cease to be difficulties at all as soon as we remember that God's providence extends over all.[12]

Yes, there are great mysteries, and we will look at these mysteries later on. But what should comfort us now as we view the world in all its turmoil, as we view the church in all its troubles, as we view

---

[12] Warfield, B.B. (2005) 'God's Providence Over All.' In: *Selected Shorter Writings*. P&R Publishing, Philippsburg: USA. Vol. 1, pp.111.

our own lives with our difficulties and trials, is that the doctrine of providence is the doctrine that brings strength and comfort to our hearts.

May God bless to us his Word.

~ 2 ~

The Working of Providence

And we know that all things work together for good to them that love God ...   Romans 8:28

We have to rest in God's wisdom, particularly in his timing of his providence. We think, in our so-called wisdom, that this is the right time for something to happen. But God's time is different. Our time is not the proper season to receive mercy. God has his kindness, as we shall see, in the working out of his purpose of grace. The delay of our mercy is really for our advantage. The Lord will 'wait, that he might be gracious' (Isaiah 30:18). Sometimes, as Thomas Boston says, we try to pluck the fruit from the tree of providence before it is ready. He says that fruit plucked from the tree of providence ere it is ripe will last a short while but set our teeth on edge while we have it.[13] Trying to make things happen according to our own time is not something that we ought to be doing. We are to wait for God's fulfilment of all his purposes and all his plans. And therefore we are to wait upon God's wisdom, and submit to God's sovereignty.

Now I thought it would be profitable for us to look at some scriptural examples of how the providence of God works. It is one thing for us to read about this in a book and to talk about it in a doctrinal way, to bring together all the truths about God's providence, but let us think of one or two examples of how it works out in the biblical narrative.

I want to think of three examples in the Scriptures that bring before us different aspects of the providence of God.

---

[13] Boston, T. (1863) *The Crook in the Lot*. Porteous and Hislop, Glasgow. p.51.

1. Esther

The first example is the Book of Esther. That is an amazing book. We are talking about the God of providence and yet in the whole book of Esther the name of God is not mentioned. Yet you could say that in a sense the whole book is filled with God, for in this book God is working out his purposes with regard to redemption, with regard to his people, and with regard to his glory, and he is doing it in a marvellous way. His name is not mentioned, but that has an effect in itself, to show us that the whole of life is under the control of God.

You remember the story of Esther. It is set in the country of Persia and it concerns the Jews in that country who had not returned to Jerusalem after the captivity. They were scattered throughout the Persian empire. Ahasuerus the king of Persia gives a huge feast, and in this feast he is displaying his wealth and his power. He wants to put Queen Vashti on display, and because she refuses to be put on display she is deposed. Ahasuerus begins to look for another queen. All the beauties in the Persian empire are rounded up and the one who is chosen happens to be this Jewish girl, Esther. People do not recognise or know that she is Jewish, but she is chosen as queen for Ahasuerus. She has a cousin, Mordecai, who is going to feature in this story. The king delights in this girl Esther and he makes her his queen.

Now another man comes into the picture—Haman. He is aspiring to be next to the king, to be first under King Ahasuerus. He wants everyone to respect him and to bow to him. But there is one man who will not do obeisance to him, and that man is Mordecai the Jew. Mordecai thinks it would be idolatry to bow down to this man, so he refuses to do it. Because Mordecai will not bow down to Haman, Haman aspires to plot the destruction of the whole Jewish race. In his fury about Mordecai's unwillingness to bow to him he is aspiring to destroy the whole Jewish race. But the superstition in that country insists that he must choose a lucky day in which to do this. How like the world this is! If you are going to do it, do it on a lucky day! So Haman chooses a day eleven months off in order to get a lucky day to destroy the Jewish race. Haman accuses the Jews of being a rebellious people and he wants the people around them to plunder the Jews and to kill them. He asks King Ahasuerus for this to be done and the king gives his assent. So this great plot is set up.

But unknown to the people and unknown to Haman, there is Esther the Jew and she is queen, and she has access to the king. She ventures in to the king to make her request. This comes out of the conversation between Esther and Mordecai, because Mordecai is concerned for what is going to happen to his people. He encourages Esther to go in to the king on behalf of their people. He says to Esther, 'If you don't do it, then enlargement and deliverance will come from another source. But God has placed you in this position in order for you to do this work.'

King Ahasuerus provides an audience for Esther and Esther invites the king and Haman to a banquet. When a second invitation is given to Haman, Haman thinks that he is being flattered and he thinks that this is his opportunity to get rid of Mordecai. So before he goes to the banquet he builds a gallows on which he is going to hang Mordecai.

But that night in the palace of Ahasuerus, the king could not sleep. When he could not sleep he calls for the records of the kingdom, and there he finds that Mordecai had warned the king about a plot. Two men who were near to Ahasuerus in his palace had plotted to kill him. Mordecai found out about this and he told the king, and those two men were beheaded. But then king Ahasuerus asked, 'What honour has been done to the man who warned me about these two men?' And the answer was that nothing had been done. So when Haman came to the king, Ahasuerus says to him, 'What shall be done to the man whom the king delights to honour?' Haman suggests that he should be given such and such honours and be paraded around the city and all this kind of thing. Ahasuerus then announces to Haman that the man who was going to have this honour is none other than Mordecai! So Haman has to see Mordecai being honoured in place of himself.

Then Esther hosts the king and Haman at the second banquet, and at this banquet she tells the king about what is going to be done to her people, the Jewish race—they are going to be destroyed. The king asks, 'Who is this wicked person that is going to destroy the whole of your people?' The answer from Esther is, 'This Haman!'

Haman is terrified. He recognises what danger he is in and he falls before the queen pleading for his life. When Ahasuerus sees this, he is all the more enraged. 'Will you insult the queen as well as doing these other things?' Ahasuerus orders that Haman be hanged on the gallows that he had prepared for Mordecai. The result of all this is that Mordecai is appointed ruler in place of Haman. The king holds out his sceptre to Esther again, and gives her permission for Mordecai to send out a decree throughout the whole of the empire that the Jews should not be destroyed, but that the Jews should be armed and they should defend themselves against those who tried to destroy them.

That is an amazing story in which the Jewish race are saved. To commemorate that wonderful deliverance of the Jewish race they appointed the Feast of Purim, which is held to this day.

a. Providence works unawares

The Book of Esther is full of the providence of God. Every aspect of the story is coming together for one glorious purpose and end, and that is to save the blood royal, to save the Jewish people. We see a great empire, and a powerful king, and the high ones in that empire. They are involved in events pertaining to the kingdom of God, but they know nothing about it. They are totally unaware of what is happening in the kingdom of God, but nevertheless they are part of this whole story. We see men and women like Haman acting freely according to their character, and yet they are in the hand of God and they are fulfilling his purposes. 'The king's heart is in the hand of God as the rivers of water and he turneth it whithersoever he will.' (Proverbs 20:1) Ahasuerus was a heathen king, but God was working through him. Haman was a wicked man, but God was working through him. They had no concern for God whatever but yet God was using them to fulfil his purposes.

b. Providence subverts evil intentions

The second thing we see in Esther's story is that the most powerful means used for the destruction of God's people are rendered ineffective. Haman thought it was all down to luck, that his lucky day had come. He was going to get rid of this man Mordecai and destroy all the Jewish people. But it turned out in the providence of God that it was he himself who was destroyed and all the people of God saved. The tables were turned in the justice and righteousness of God. God can do that, and God does that. He is overturning the purposes of the wicked and he is advancing his own cause in the very ways in which the wicked are working.

We see this of course in the way in which evil men and Satan are persecuting the church of Jesus Christ. You think that is working to the disadvantage of the church? God is rendering it effective to the advance of the church. The blood of the martyrs is the seed of the church. Patrick Hamilton the Reformer was burnt at the stake because of his desire for pure doctrine and pure worship, and the authorities were also going to burn other people who stood for the truth in

Scotland. It was said by someone to the Archbishop in Scotland at that time, 'My lord, if you will burn them, let them be burned in the deepest cellars, for the smoke of Master Patrick's burning has infected as many as it blew upon.' They were trying to suppress the Reformation. They were trying to suppress the work of God. They put a man to death, burning him at the stake. Yet that did more for the Reformation than anything else. The wicked thought that they were prospering and that they were hindering the work of God, but it turned out to be the very opposite, because the martyrdom of Patrick Hamilton was the means by which many others came to an understanding of the Reformed faith and took courage and stood up for that very faith. So you see God renders ineffective the wickedness of man and he turns people's evil purposes and plans to the advantage of the church and of his cause.[14]

---

[14] Mr Murray also recommended William Plumer's treatment of Judas Iscariot in his book, *Jehovah-Jireh: A Treatise on Providence*. He commented, 'One interesting chapter is entirely devoted to the case of Judas Iscariot — a great mystery in the providence of God! How such a

c. Providence times things perfectly

Also in the story of Esther we see how things fall out in the nick of time. Things happen at precisely the right point to fulfil God's plans and purposes. There are seven points in the book of Esther, developments in the work of providence, where you could say that if any one had failed at one moment the whole story would have been different. All the events are working precisely together for the end that God has in view. Why was it that on that one night of all nights the king could not sleep? It was in the providence of God. He purposed it. Why was there no reward for what Mordecai had done? Why was there no recognition of it in the records? Because it was in the providence of God. Because it had to be accomplished at a certain time.

---

wicked a man was amongst the disciples of the Lord Jesus Christ and what happened in his life and how perhaps the greatest sin that was ever committed in betraying the Lord Jesus Christ, his Master and his Lord! Yet this turned out in the providence of God to bring about the greatest event in the salvation of mankind. I found that chapter very helpful and very solemn.'

Humanly speaking, if one act of providence in that whole sequence of events had failed then the story would have turned out differently. But God is working it all out. His timing is perfect. He brings everything to fruition in his own time. God's time is so different from man's timing and God's purposes are being worked out by God bringing together all kinds of different providences and working them out just as he pleases and in his own time.

So Esther is a picture of providence working on a grand scale. Providence is working in the world, for the church and for the people of God in particular. Providence causes nations to be involved in the ongoing work of redemption, for the work of redemption involves Christ's kingship over the nations.

2. Joseph

Another example is Joseph. As you know, Joseph was the son of Rachel by Jacob. His mother had died in childbirth, so he was brought up without a mother, and he was his father's favourite son. But because he was his father's favourite son, his brothers hated him.

Joseph also had great dreams about the future and about what greatness was going to come to him. His brothers envied him. They conspired against him and even wanted to kill him. They cast him into a pit and then sold him to the Ishmaelites. The Ishmaelites sold him to Potiphar, an officer in Pharaoh's household in Egypt. Joseph became successful in that household, but he was subjected to a great temptation. Potiphar's wife falsely accused him and so he was cast into prison.

He lay there in prison and he must have wondered what God was doing with him. The butler and the baker had dreams in the prison and Joseph was able to interpret those dreams. The interpretation was to the advantage of the butler and to the disadvantage of the baker. The butler was restored to Pharaoh's palace, and he promised that he would speak about Joseph to Pharaoh. But he forgot all about it and it was not until some years later, when Pharaoh had a dream he did not understand, that the butler suddenly remembered about the man he had met in prison who was able to interpret dreams. So he told Pharaoh about him and Joseph was brought out of prison to interpret Pharaoh's dream.

The meaning of Pharaoh's dream was that there would be seven years of plenty followed by seven years of famine. The famine was going to cover the whole area, and all the countries in that area would come to Egypt in order to find grain to eat. Because of his interpretation of the dream, Joseph was made prime minister in Egypt.

After a while, when the famine took hold, Joseph's brothers came to Egypt in order to find food. Of course, Joseph recognised them, and he tested them and tried them before he revealed himself to them. There was a great reunion with his brothers, and after that with his father. Joseph arranged for his father to come down to Egypt, with the whole family. They settled in the land of Goshen and they multiplied.

After seventeen years in the land of Egypt, Jacob died. Joseph's brothers thought that he would take vengeance against them. They thought, 'We did a terrible thing to him, therefore he will get his own back on us.' But Joseph had no intention of getting his own back on his brothers. He said to them, 'Ye planned evil, but God meant it for good.' What an amazing picture of the sovereignty of God and the providence of God! The brothers were being used by God through their hatred and jealousy of Joseph. After all these years Joseph has come to this conclusion, 'You planned it for evil, but God meant it for good. God sent me before you to preserve your posterity in the earth and to save your lives by a great deliverance.' So, he said, 'it wasn't you that sent me hither but God.'

Again we see the providence of God working on a grand scale. It was twenty-two years from the time that Joseph was cast into the pit by his brothers before the providences of God were manifested in that Joseph had been sent to Egypt to save the people of God by providing grain for them.

a. Providence can seem to contradict the promises

The thing in particular we see in Joseph's life is that the providences of God seemed to be going against the promises of God. God had told Joseph by dreams (which was a usual way for God to reveal something to his people in those days) that he was going to have his brothers bowing down to him, that he was going to be a great man, that he was going to be a man of great influence. But everything in the providence of God seemed to be going against this. First of all he was cast into a pit, then he was cast into prison, and he languished there in prison. He was laid in irons, as we sang in Psalm 105, or, as it could be translated, the iron entered into his soul. That was the darkest hour in the experience of Joseph. Why was he kept in prison? Psalm 105 tells us, 'until the time that God's word came: the word of the Lord tried him.'

You see, there was a conflict. God's Word had spoken to him and said that he was going to experience great things and he was going to be an influential man. But here in prison his experience seemed to contradict God's Word. Everything seemed to be against God's Word. God's providence seemed to be against God's Word! But this was only 'until the time that the Lord's word came.' There was a time in which God had planned to deliver him, and the moment that time came, the prison could not hold him, because it was God's time for his liberty. God's time came and loosed him, and the king made him ruler over all his kingdom. He was exalted from the prison to be prime minister.

That is the amazing providence of God. It is always a trial of faith as far as we are concerned. Abraham experienced it. He was asked to offer up his only son, Isaac. God had promised Abraham that he was going to have a son and this son was going to be the one in whom all the nations of the earth were going to be blessed. Yet God tells him to offer up this son. 'Take your son, your only son Isaac, and offer him up for a sacrifice.' That is the trial of faith. Abraham obeyed God. He went forth and he bound his son to the altar. He was about to raise the knife when God calls from heaven and Abraham's faith was rewarded. God provided another sacrifice.

Dark providences try our faith, and yet we are to wait upon God until we see (after some time, it may be) what God means in the darkness of providence. Joseph could look back on his time in the prison and say, 'This is what God had in mind. He was preparing me for something great and glorious. I had to pass through this, and it wasn't easy to understand while I was passing through it, but now I see it all.' John Flavel says that providences, like the Hebrew language, have to be read backwards. You cannot say that this or that is going to happen or why it is going to happen. But when it has happened, you look back on your life and on your trials and on your difficulties and the dark providences you went through, and you say, 'Oh, that was God's purpose for me. That is what God was doing for me in that dark providence. He had a purpose in it and now I see it. I couldn't see it at the time, but I can see it now.'

b. Providence transforms and purifies us

The other thing I would like to say on Joseph is that God's providence is not only something that tries us but also something that tests us. God's providences in our lives, including the dark providences, are things that build character. If you ever found a spoilt child in all the world, it was Joseph. He had come from a very difficult family background and a very difficult situation—his father's favourite son, without a mother, with strange brothers who belonged to the family. When he came forth from his father's house he was certainly not fit to be a leader. He certainly was not fit to be a prime minister. But God worked on his character. By adversity God shaped him and God proved him and God tried him. And when he was tried he came forth as gold.

The dark providences that we pass through as children of God are God's engine, as it were, to change us. They are God's fires, to refine us and purify us and make us what we should be. For example, Joseph's own father Jacob was a deceiver and a twister. He deceived his brother Esau. What did God do? He sent him to Laban his uncle, where he served for fourteen years, and Laban deceived him. The one who deceived others became subject to deception himself. God put him through the fire and God changed his character. We can say now that the God of Jacob is our refuge because he is the God who transforms the character of his people and changes their lives and makes them to be what they are.

Another interesting thing about Jacob is this. Remember when Joseph was in the process of revealing himself to his brothers, his father Jacob back home still thought that Joseph was dead and that he had lost Simeon in Egypt. When the brothers came back to Jacob to tell him what had happened in their latest journey to Egypt, Jacob said, 'All these things are against me.' 'Joseph is dead, Simeon is kept in Egypt, now they are taking Benjamin away too. All these things are against me.' That is how we speak in ignorance, without knowing the true work and purpose of God. At that very moment when Jacob said, 'All these things are against me,' they were actually all working for his good! Joseph was still alive, Simeon was safe, and so was Benjamin. Soon Jacob would be reunited with his son that he thought was dead, and there would be abundant provision for him and for all the people of God!

Sometimes we will be in that situation. We shall have all kinds of difficulties and trials. We will not know where to turn and we will say to ourselves, 'All these things are against me!' But the glorious thing is that if we are a child of God, we can be assured that these things are all working together for good, because God's purposes for his children are always good.

> Ill that he blesses is our good,
>   and unblest good is ill;
> And all is right that seems most wrong,
>   if it be his sweet will.

(F. W. Faber)

That is the way that providence works in the people of God.

3. Job

In the case of Esther we have seen the providence of God, in the mystery of it, working on a national scale in which God preserves his church and his people. We have also seen providence working in an individual like Joseph and how God works out his purposes for his people even when it seems most unlikely. I want to look at one more example, and that is the example of Job.

If we want to think of a situation that brings before us the mystery of suffering then we have to go to the Book of Job. This is outlined for us in chapter 1 of Job. God says to Satan, 'Have you considered my servant Job? There is none like him in the earth, a perfect and an upright man, one that feareth God and escheweth evil.' Then Satan answered the Lord and said, 'Doth Job fear God for nothing? Hast thou not made a hedge about him and about his house and about all that he has on every side?'

What Satan is saying in effect is that Job is what is sometimes called 'a rice Christian.' He is only in it for what he can get out of it. He is serving God because it is in his best interests to serve God. God has prospered him therefore it is to his advantage to be a Christian. That is what Satan is accusing Job of.

Now God as it were puts Job on display. He says to Satan, 'Behold, all that he hath is in thy power, only upon himself put not forth thine hand.' So Satan went forth from the presence of God. And one tragedy after another comes upon Job. We cannot go into them tonight—you know the things that happened in his life. But what is Job's reaction? Well, Job bows down and worships. 'The Lord gave, and the Lord hath taken away: blessed be the name of the Lord.' Job refuses to go in with Satan and to accuse God of injustice. His wife is of a different mind, but Job stands firm. He does not change his view of God. He does not lose his integrity. He goes through all the sufferings that come to his belongings and to his family and ultimately to his person. All these difficulties fall upon him and then his false friends come along.

a. Dark providences are explained by God's sovereignty

And is there an answer in the end for Job's sufferings? Well, there is not an answer. The only answer that Job gets is, 'Where were you when I laid the foundation of the earth?' In other words, God gives Job a display of his sovereignty in creation. An implication is this that we only know as creatures. God alone knows as the Creator. The answer that comes to Job is the sovereignty of God—the fact that he has a right to do what he wills with his own.

You see, this is the account of Job's suffering. God has chosen this godly man to be a battlefield, as it were, between heaven and earth. Satan wants to prove that Job is a Christian just for what he can get out of it. God is putting Job on display as a man who loves God for who he is and not for what he receives from him. In other words, Job's love for God is genuine. It is true. He loves God for who he is, and not for what he can get out of God.

That is the great test and trial that is going on in the book of Job. His sufferings cannot be accounted for by anything in his own life. David had many sufferings in his life—many afflictions, many trials—because he had sinned. He had committed adultery and he committed murder and God's hand of chastisement was upon David from that moment on. David knew it: he could testify to the fact that God was afflicting him for his sin. God will afflict us for our sins. But Job kept his integrity. There was no specific sin that Job was guilty of, but yet he was a man who suffered in this terrible way. You can only account for his sufferings because God is putting him on display. 'Have you considered my servant Job, that there is none like him in all the earth?' Satan is allowed, as it were, to test Job, to try Job, and Job comes out in the end purified as pure gold. He comes through the fire of suffering and testing.

b. Dark providences have a greater purpose

You see, the providence of God is working in our sufferings as well as the rest of our lives. There is mystery in it. We cannot account for everything that happens in people's lives. There is a danger that when we see people suffering affliction we are ready to point the finger and to say, 'O there must be some sin in their life. They must have done something that God is chastising them for, something that God is afflicting them for.' That could be a completely wrong analysis. There may be other reasons why God in his providence is sending dark things into a person's life. He did in the case of Job. He does in many of his people. Perhaps it is in order to bring about greater usefulness in the kingdom of God. That may be the reason why some men or some women are going through greater times of difficulty than others— because God is making them so that they will have greater usefulness.

Think of Charles Haddon Spurgeon, the great preacher in London in the nineteenth century. He had tremendous physical suffering and mental depression. He spent so much time out of the pulpit, and he had to go to the south of France time and time again to recover his health. His wife was unwell too, bedridden. Yet from her sick bed she was exercising a ministry. She set up the Book Fund, through which she supplied books to ministers all over the United Kingdom. Here are two people greatly afflicted by God, unaccountably afflicted by God, and yet what is the outcome of it? Tremendous fruitfulness.

What a tremendous impact Spurgeon had in his day! What a tremendous influence he had as a preacher of the gospel, and as a writer! All his sermons were printed weekly and went out through the whole country and overseas, feeding people's souls, even though he himself was very often lying prostrate on his bed or away in the south of France under severe physical and mental affliction. But you see, God was doing it. God's providence was doing it, and it was bringing a richness into his life and others were receiving a blessing.

That is one of the ways in which providence works—not just that we may receive a blessing ourselves, but that we might become a blessing to others. We go through the mill and through trials and tribulations, but God has a greater purpose. Today Spurgeon's sermons and books are being published all throughout the world, and he is feeding the souls of God's people in the most remote parts of the world. People who haven't got a ministry of the Word, a pastoral ministry, are being fed upon the sermons and the writings of Charles Haddon Spurgeon. This fruitfulness can be traced back to God's dealings with his servant in providence.

So we see in these areas of Scripture and the lives of the people of God how providence is working, and particularly in the dark providences.

I will end with a quote from Ralph Erskine. He speaks about these dark providences and God's purpose in the dark providences. This is how he says it:

> It is to discover himself [make himself known] in a way suitable to himself, and his glorious perfections, and to show that his thoughts are not our thoughts, nor his ways our ways. If he should

work according to our thoughts and imaginations, how would it appear that he is Jehovah and sovereign God that acts like himself?[15]

God owes us no explanations, but we owe him implicit trust and obedience. It is not easy to trust God when he appears to be silent, as he was with Job, but trust we must.

You see, he is a God who does wonders. He works through these dark providences to bring about the glory of his name and to further his praise. His way is in the sea and his path in the deep waters. We cannot understand it at this time, but when it comes forth then we see the wonder of it. Part of our blessedness here upon earth and the great blessedness in the world to come will be looking back on our lives and seeing the marvellous providences of God. These will be material for our praise in time and in eternity.

---

[15] Erskine, R. (1821) *Sermons and other Practical Works*. R. Baynes, London. Vol. 7, p.14.

~ 3 ~

The Beauty of Providence

Let them exalt him also in the congregation of the people, and praise him in the assembly of the elders. ... [42]The righteous shall see it, and rejoice: and all iniquity shall stop her mouth. [43]Whoso is wise, and will observe these things, even they shall understand the lovingkindness of the LORD.

Psalm 107:33-43

We are considering the mystery of providence, and we turn now to the observation of it and delight in it. Psalm 107 is recounting to us the works of the Lord. We have four pictures in this Psalm of God's dealings with the children of men, and each section of the Psalm ends with the refrain, 'Oh that men would praise the Lord for his goodness, and for his wonderful works to the children of men!'

As we come to the end of Psalm 107 we have in verses 33-41 an indication of what God is doing in the world—how he is acting according to his own plan and purpose, how he is overthrowing and establishing, how he is casting down and building up. All these things are manifestations of how God is working in the world. Then we come down to verse 43. As we reflect upon these things, as we see these things happening, the psalmist says to us, 'the righteous shall see it and rejoice, and all iniquity shall stop her mouth.' All these things that are happening in the world will be a source of joy and rejoicing to the people of God, to the church of God. At the same time it will be a rebuke to the wicked. Iniquity shall stop her mouth. These are the marvellous things that happen when we remember and contemplate and see the providence of God in what he is doing in the world.

The Psalmist ends on this note: 'whoso is wise, and will observe these things, even they shall understand the lovingkindness of the Lord.' There is a duty laid before us in this verse. We are to observe the providences of God. We are to observe the works of God. He has laid them out before us in order that we may look at them, observe them, take note of them, meditate upon them.

There is a qualification. 'Whoso is wise will observe these things.' We need wisdom. We need heavenly wisdom, we need divine wisdom. The world does not look at these things. They think that it all happens by chance. But the children of God are those who are made wise by God himself, and part of the wisdom they are given from God is that they are observing the providences of God. They are looking at what God is doing in the world.

And what is the benefit that they are going to receive? They are going to understand the lovingkindness of the Lord. As they view the providence of God, as they observe it and as they see God's workings in his church and to his people, and to them as individuals, they are going to see the lovingkindness of the Lord. There is going to be a demonstration and a manifestation of the lovingkindness of the Lord.

Speaking on this verse the Scottish theologian Thomas Boston says:

> Whoever would walk with God must be due observers of the Word and providences of God, for by these in a special manner he manifests himself to his people. In the one [the Word] we see what he says; in the other what he does. These are the two books that every student of holiness ought to be much conversant in. They are both written with the one hand and they should both be carefully read by those who would have not only the name of religion but the thing itself. They should be studied together if we would profit by either, for being taken together, they give light one to the other, and as it is our duty to read the Word, so also it is our duty to observe the works of God.[16]

There Thomas Boston is telling us the two areas that we are to observe. We are to observe God in his Word and to observe God in his providence, his works.

---

[16] Boston, T. (1848) *An Illustration of the Doctrines of the Christian Religion with respect to Faith and Practice.* George and Robert King, Aberdeen. Vol 1, p.193.

1. Ways of observing providence

I want to speak first of all about the two-fold revelation. One part of it is the revelation of God in his Word. There is a transcendent and glorious manifestation of God in his Word, and that manifestation of course is through the one who God has sent into this world, the Lord Jesus Christ, the brightness of his glory and the express image of his person. There in the Word we behold the glory of God—the nature of God, the character of God. But also there is a manifestation of God in his providence. We are to look at that manifestation of God in his providence. We are to observe the works of God.

What is the providence of God really doing? Well, the providences of God are fulfilling the Word of God. The Word of God is full of plans and purposes, of God taking counsel, of God planning things and promising things. He promises many things in his Word. How do we see these things fulfilled? We see them fulfilled in the providences of God, in the works of God.

The primary glory and excellency of his providential works consist in this, that they are the very fulfillings and real accomplishments of his written Word. By a wise and heedful attendance hereunto we might often clear the mysterious occurrences of providences by reducing them to the written Word, and there lodge them as effects in their proper causes. Doubtless this is one of the wisest methods men could pursue against atheism, to show how providences concur in a most obvious tendency to confirm this great conclusion, 'Thy word is truth.' [17]

God has told us his plans and given us his promises, and as we see these fulfilled in the history of redemption in the Scriptures, we can see that God's Word is true. We have to have special respect to the Word of God being fulfilled as we view the works of God.

Solomon in his prayer acknowledges the promises and providences of God. He tells us in 1 Kings 8:24 that the promises and providences of God went

---

[17] Flavel, J. (1820) 'Divine Conduct; or, the Mystery of Providence.' In: *The Whole Works of Rev. Mr. John Flavel.* Baynes and Son, London. Vol. 4, p.339.

along step by step with his father all his days, and that God's hand had fulfilled that which his mouth had spoken. God had spoken promises to Solomon, and these promises were being fulfilled, and therefore God's Word was being confirmed. And so Joshua in like manner acknowledged this. 'Not one thing has failed of all the good things which the Lord your God spake concerning you' (Joshua 23:14). He carefully observed the relation of the works of God to the Word of God and there was an exact harmony between God's Word and God's works.

God's Word and God's works work in harmony. This is how Flavel puts it:

> If two men travel along one road it is agreed that they are likely to go to the same place. Providence and Scripture go all one way and if they seem at times to go different or opposite ways be sure they will meet at the journey's end. There is an agreement between them to do so.[18]

That is a good illustration for us. Providence and Scripture are going in the same direction. God's

18 *Ibid.* p.359.

promises and the fulfilment of them are going in the same direction. At times they appear to be going in opposite directions. That is the mystery of providence, when the one seems to be contradicting the other. But, says Flavel, 'there is an agreement between them.' The agreement is that they are going to meet at the end of the day, and what God has promised will assuredly be fulfilled. His providence will ensure that his Word is fulfilled.

That is the reason why we should have such confidence in the providence of God. We should have full confidence that God is working everything according to his plan and purpose and that he will fulfil all that he has purposed and all that he has promised at the end of the day. So the providences of God are fulfilling the Word of God. This is another, rather quaint, illustration that the Puritans used. Promises, they said, are like a pregnant woman. She must accomplish her appointed months and when she has done so providence like the midwife brings these mercies into the world.[19] There is a time in which God is

---

[19] For example, John Flavel, *Ibid*. p.472.

working. He has made his plan, he has given his promise, and there is a waiting for these promises. But when things are being fulfilled these promises are brought to fruition. They are big with mercy. The exhortation to the saints is to take courage:

> The clouds you so much dread
> Are filled with mercy, and shall break
> with blessings on your head.
>
> (*William Cowper*)

There may be clouds on the horizon, dark clouds, but these clouds are full of blessing, like the clouds are full of rain. And when God's time comes these clouds will break and they will break with blessing on your head. God's Word is being fulfilled by God's providences.

a. Providence is interpreted by the Word

It is important for us to remember that the Word is always our guide to providence. As we think of the providences of God there is perhaps a danger for us to misinterpret the leadings of providences. You think of Lot, the nephew of Abraham. He was given the choice of the land to which he was to go and he saw the rich and fertile valley that went towards the way of Sodom. He must have thought, 'Surely this is the providence of God! God is giving me the opportunity to have such a rich place to feed my flocks and to look after my family!' He looked at the providence and the providence seemed good and he followed the providence. But he was wrong. The providence seemingly pointed to Sodom, but Lot was sadly mistaken. Abraham made the right choice. He put God first and the things of eternity first, but Lot put the things of this world first. To look at the providence without consulting the Word can lead in the wrong direction.

Also think of David. Remember when Saul was pursuing David. The time came in that pursuit where Saul went into a cave and David was in that cave, and David had the opportunity to kill Saul. That would be the end, you would think, of all his troubles and all his difficulties! What an opportunity laid to his hand! The man who was pursuing him ready to kill him is there and he just needs to kill him! That is what providence might have directed him to, if we look at it in that way, but it was the Word that was controlling David, not the providence. He said, 'How can I lay hands upon the Lord's anointed?'

We will be faced with choices in life. It may be that something has come into our life, some relationship perhaps, and it seems to direct us that we should go in a certain way, because this is how things are turning out. But what must govern us in our choices first and foremost is the Word of God. That is our direction. We are not directed by providence in the sense of it leading and guiding us. As we fulfil the Word and obey the Word then we will see providences working out. But providence is not to be our main guide. The Word is to be our main guide and we are to be directed by the Word.

'Providence without the Word,' says William Plumer, 'is a dark enigma. None can solve it. The best commentary on providence is the Bible. The best commentary on the Bible is providence. The events of a good man's life are to him the fulfillings of the Scriptures.'[20]

---

[20] *Ibid*. pp.140-141.

b. Providence is sanctified by grace

Another thing we are to remember is this. Providences without the influence of divine grace on the heart do not have a sanctifying influence, even on good men. We need the sanctifying influences of grace to make providences blessed to us.

We need to have providences blessed to us. Providences happen in the nation. Providences happen to the church. Providences happen to individuals. God sends certain things into our lives, like sickness for example, and sometimes we do not acknowledge the hand of God in these things. We do not see the purpose of God in sending them. We do not seek the blessing of God upon them and they are not sanctified to us.

Therefore there is the necessity of grace in order that these providences that God sends into our lives are sanctified and blessed to us.

2. Ways of reflecting on providence

Secondly, we think of the reflection that we are to have upon providence. We are to observe providence. 'Whoso is wise, and will observe these things, even they shall understand the lovingkindness of the Lord.'

What kind of reflection should we have upon providence? John Flavel makes a distinction. There is first of all what he calls an 'entire and full' reflection. That is, the whole complex and perfect system of providence when it is all worked out. He says,

> This blessed sight is reserved for the perfect state. It is in that mount of God where we shall see both the wilderness and Canaan, the glorious kingdom into which we are come and the way through which we were led into it. There the saints will have a ravishing view of it in its entirety, and every part shall be distinctly discerned, as it had its particular use, and as it was connected with other parts, and how effectually and orderly they all wrought to bring about that blessed design of their salvation according to the promise, 'And we know that all things work together for good to

THE MYSTERY OF PROVIDENCE

them that love God, to them who are the called
according to his purpose' (Romans 8:28).[21]

When Dr Martyn Lloyd-Jones died in 1981, his
funeral service was held in his native Wales in a
place called Newcastle Emlyn. One of the hymns
that was sung at that funeral is a very touching
hymn. It was originally written in Welsh, and one
of the verses in English translation is this:

> From heavenly Jerusalem's tower,
> Their path through the desert they trace;
> And every affliction they suffered
> Redounds to the glory of grace.
>
> (*David Charles*)

Here are the saints of God, and they have reached
the heavenly Jerusalem. They are looking back on
their journey through the wilderness—'their path
through the desert they trace'—and what do they
discover? Every affliction they suffered redounds to
the glory of grace. God will have all the glory at the
end of the day. Everything that happened to the
saints was in the purpose and plan of God, and part

---

[21] *Ibid*. p.348.

of the blessedness of heaven will indeed be their contemplation of the way that God led them. This is what Flavel says:

> Oh how ravishing and delectable a sight it will be to behold at one view the whole design of providence, and the proper place and use of every single act, which we could not understand in this world! What Christ said to Peter is as applicable to some providences in which we are concerned as it was to that particular action: 'What I do, thou knowest not now, but thou shalt know hereafter.' All the dark, intricate, puzzling providences at which we were sometimes so offended, and sometimes amazed, which we could neither reconcile with the promise nor with each other, nay, which we so unjustly censured and bitterly bewailed, as if they had fallen out quite against our happiness, we shall then see to be to us, as the difficult passage through the wilderness was to Israel, 'the right way to the city of habitation.'[22]

So the entire and full reflection on providence has to await the end of this life. It has to await the great day of Christ's second coming.

---

[22] *Op. cit.*

What then are we to do in the meantime? Well, says John Flavel, there is a 'partial and imperfect' reflection upon providence. He says,

> The other side is impartial and imperfect, which we have on the way to glory, during which we only view it in its single acts, or, at most, in some branches and more observable series of actions.[23]

Between the entire and full reflection that we will have in glory and the partial and imperfect reflection we have here upon earth, Flavel says, is the same difference as between 'the sight of the disjointed wheels and scattered pins of a watch and the sight of the whole united in one frame and working in one orderly motion.'[24] You see a watch repairer, and he takes a watch to bits. It is lying there on his bench and you wonder what on earth this is going to be like? How can all these parts really make a watch that is going to keep time? That is what it is like viewing providence here on this earth.

---

[23] *Op. cit.*
[24] *Op. cit.*

Alternatively, Flavel says,

> [It is like the difference] between an ignorant
> spectator who views some more observable vessel
> or joint of a dissected body, and the accurate
> anatomist who discerns the course of all the veins
> and arteries of the body as he follows the various
> branches of them through the whole, and plainly
> sees the proper place, figure and use of each, with
> their mutual respect to one another.[25]

That is the difference. And so there is a walking
with God in this world, in which we see in part, we
see through a glass darkly. But even in that
reflection there is a sweet communion with God.
There is communion with God in his Word, and we
are to cultivate that communion. There is a
meditation on God's Word that leads us to
communion and fellowship with God. But over and
above the communion we have with God through
his Word, we have communion with God in his
providence. We find the excellence and sweetness
in God's dealings with us as his children. Jacob
called his Bethel the gate of heaven. And as we look

---

[25] *Op. cit.*

at the providences in our lives we see the lovingkindness of the Lord, and these providences become to us Bethel, the very gate of heaven, and through them we have sweet communion with God.

And so there is that two-fold reflection upon the providences of God. We are to observe them. We are to observe them in this life. It is part of our duty, our responsibility if we are to be wise as the children of God to do that. And so there is a two-fold revelation: Word and providence. There is a two-fold reflection, entire and complete at the end of the day which will be the material of praise for him, and there is this partial reflection that we have during our wilderness journey in this life.

3. Ways of delighting in providence

But then the third thing we are to think about is the delight that we are to have in these reflections on providence. John Flavel goes on to demonstrate that the great power of the pleasures and delights of the Christian life is made out in the observation of providence. He quotes Psalm 111:2. 'The works of the Lord are great, sought out of all them that have pleasure therein.' The study of the works of God in providence ought to give us pleasure. This is what Flavel says:

> Oh what a world of rarities is to be found in providence! The blind, heedless world makes nothing of them. They cannot find one sweet bit where a gracious soul would make a rich feast. ... Had a spiritual and wise Christian had the dissecting and anatomising of such a work of providence, what glory it would have yielded to God! What comfort and encouragement to the soul![26]

And he uses this illustration:

> The bee makes a sweeter meal upon one single flower than the ox does upon the whole field where thousands of these flowers grow.[27]

The Christian makes a sweeter feast on one single flower than the world can make on thousands. The Christian may see something marvellous in one

---

[26] *Ibid.* p.341.
[27] *Op. cit.*

providence, which the world cannot see in a multitude of providences.

It is interesting for us to think that many of the Puritans who wrote treatises on providence and related subjects kept diaries. I do not know if any of you keep a diary, but the Puritans were very strong on keeping diaries—keeping records of God's goodness to you in your life. I believe that John Flavel kept a diary, but unfortunately that diary has never seen the light of day. Who knows but it might possibly turn up in someone's attic somewhere in England! He was minister in Dartmouth in the south of England. What a blessed thing it would be to find the diary of John Flavel!

Flavel makes this exhortation to us:

> Histories are usually read with delight. When once the fancy is touched, a man does not know how to disengage himself from it. I am greatly mistaken if the history of our own lives, if it were well drawn up and distinctly perused, would not be the pleasantest history that ever we read in our lives. … But, reader, thou only art able to compile the history of providence for thyself, because the memorials that furnish it are only in thine own

hands. However, here thou mayest find a pattern,
and general rule to direct thee…[28]

The pattern and rule Flavel is referring to is his own
work. He is writing this work on providence to help
people to compile for themselves things that have
happened in their lives, to record them, to write
them down, to reflect upon them and then, perhaps
years later, to go back and think what a marvellous
manifestation of God's goodness it was to them in
that case. That is something that gives delight in the
Christian life.

I am going to share with you by way of conclusion
some of the things that should cause us to delight in
God and to delight in his providence as we look at
the history of the church and the history of
individual lives.

a. The instruments

For example, William Plumer says, 'God employs
such instruments as greatly confound us.' As we
look at God's providence we see so many amazing

---

[28] *Op. cit.*

things and some are things that really confound us. For instance, Plumer says,

> Will he cure Naaman's leprosy? A little captive maid shall tell him of the prophet of the Lord. Will he lead forth Israel from Egyptian bondage? That little infant in a basket among the rushes, by edict doomed to death as soon as born, shall be the deliverer. Will he make Joseph premier of Egypt? His brethren envy and sell him, the Ishmaelites carry him far from all loved ones, Potiphar imprisons him, the iron enters into his flesh; yet in God's providence every step is one onward. ... Must God's people be brought out of Babylon? Cyrus shall send forth the binding decree. The worshipper of the sun [as Cyrus was] deals as tenderly with God's people as a nurse with a child. It would not have been more wonderful to see the wolf nourishing and protecting the lamb and the kid [as to see Cyrus nursing the children of God]! Who would have supposed that God would choose a raven to feed Elijah, the boy Samuel to bear heavy tidings to Eli, or the youth Jeremiah to pull down, destroy, and build up kingdoms?[29]

---

[29] *Ibid.* pp.116-117.

Then Plumer comes over to the New Testament.

> Will God regenerate a world? It shall not be done by the ministry of angels, but to the poor, condemned, and dying, the riches of his mercy shall be borne in earthen vessels. Will God subdue the world to knowledge, to peace and righteousness? Humble men shall be his ambassadors. Will he make of his people a glorious church? Not many wise men after the flesh, not many mighty, not many noble are called: but God hath chosen the foolish things of the world to confound the wise ...[30]

These are the things that give delight to the children of God!

b. The variety

Plumer also comments on the way in which the workings of God are 'infinitely diversified, even in the midst of a general uniformity.' He says:

> He saves or he destroys in any way he pleases, by the strong, or by the weak; by friend or by foe; when danger is seen, and when it is unseen. He

---

[30] *Ibid.* pp.117-118.

sends an army of men, or an army of caterpillars to punish a guilty nation. In either case the work is done. He shakes a leaf, or sends an earthquake, and each does its errand. God is confined to no routine. He knows and commands all causes, all agents, all truths, all errors, all influences, and all oppositions. At a nod he makes the great, small; or the small, great. No mortal can tell which of two causes is the greater, till he sees what God will make of them.[31]

This is exactly what you see at the end of Psalm 107. 'God turneth rivers into a wilderness, and the water-springs into dry ground; a fruitful land into barrenness, for the wickedness of them that dwell therein. He turneth the wilderness into a standing water, and dry ground into water springs.' It all depends on the sovereignty of God and the purpose God has for men. Plumer continues, 'Men and causes are considerable or contemptible according to the fiat [the will] of Jehovah. That which to us sometimes seems like confusion is fact all order.'

---

[31] *Ibid.* pp.108.

That is the working of the providence of God that gives delight to his people.

c. The unobtrusiveness

Another area which William Plumer mentions is 'the absence of pomp and parade' in God's providence.

> How noiseless are most of God's doings! When in spring Jehovah would reanimate all nature, bring into activity myriads of insects, give growth to millions of seeds, and clothe mountains and valleys in living green, it is all a silent work. When he would subvert a universal monarchy, long before the time set for that purpose he puts it into the heart of a great ruler to build a bridge, and for that purpose to change the channel of that river for a season. This is all done without signs in heaven, or war in the elements. In the fulness of time the same river is, by means the simplest, diverted from its channel. Belshazzar is slain, Babylon is a prey to the invader, and a universal empire is dissolved.[32]

---

[32] *Ibid.* p.111.

By that simple thing, without any fuss, God does his work.

> ... There was no noise of preparation for the destruction of Sodom and Gomorrah. The morning of their eternal overthrow was as calm as any on which the sun had risen upon them.[33]

The silence in God's working, the absence of pomp and parade, is so unlike the works of men!

d. The inexplicableness

There is also a fourth area in which Plumer brings out the wonderful works of God. As he says,

> We often tremble to see God pursuing a course which to our short sight seems quite contrary to the end to be gained. This is for two purposes. The first is to humble us and thus prepare us for the reception of great blessing. The other is to prove that beside him there is no Saviour.[34]

He uses the example of the children of Israel at the Red Sea:

---

[33] *Ibid.* p.111.
[34] *Ibid.* p.119.

When mountains and waters and cruel Egyptians hedged in the Israelites on every side, and it was manifest that vain was the help of man, then came the word, 'Stand still and see the salvation of God,' and the sea was cleft in twain, and its waves became walls. 'In the mount it shall be seen' is for a saying in Israel.[35]

Here is God working in what seems contrary to the end. God brings his people to the point of despair. But in the end God intervenes. God did not send the gospel into this world 'until men had racked their inventions and were at their wits' end.'[36] After the world by wisdom knew not God, it pleased God by the foolishness of preaching to save them that believe. When the world had tried every remedy and found it wanting, God sent his Son into the world to confound the wisdom of this world.

e. The timing

Finally, Plumer speaks about how the interpositions of providence for God's people are so seasonable.

---

[35] *Op. cit.*
[36] *Op. cit.*

We mentioned something of this previously—how God's providences come in the very nick of time.

> Just as Abraham is about to make his son a sacrifice, behold a ram caught in the thicket. Just as Hagar lays down her son to die, God leads her to discover a well of water to save his life. Just as Saul is ready to seize David, and there seems to be no escape to the hunted partridge, that guilty persecutor is called home by an invasion of the Philistines.[37]

Plumer mentions other such incidents and some incidents from history that are very striking. He says,

> To sense all is dark. To mere natural reason nothing is clear. Yet [the child of God] has hope towards God. Nor is he disappointed. Enlargement and deliverance come just in time to show that none ever trusted in God and was disappointed. A seasonable mercy is a double mercy.[38]

---

[37] *Ibid*. p.142.
[38] *Ibid*. p.143.

It is like a man who is sick. He appreciates medicine more than a man who is well. And so the people of God are tried and tested and are in the furnace of affliction. They do not know how to come out, or find the way out, yet when everything seems so dark, God sends deliverance. Then that is what Plumer calls a double mercy because the person sees the wonder of God's intervention when everything else is so dark and would lead him to despair.

4. Conclusion

So that is what we are encouraged to do—observe and delight in God's providence. How far we are removed today from that kind of thing! It was so much of the delight of the Christian in days past. We have become so busy, so concerned with the things of this world, so caught up with our daily routine and the pressures that come upon us that we do not seem to have the time to read the Word as we ought to do in order to fellowship with God. Nor do we seem to have time to trace the hand of God in history. How few of us today really study history? Yet we should cultivate a love for history, and particularly the history of the church, for example in Christian biographies. How important these things are if we are going to praise God aright! Because we read in these histories the marvels that God did for his church and for his people in days past. It is not only what we have in Scripture but the ongoing work of God down through the centuries— what he did for his people in great deliverances. That is great matter of praise for us.

Psalm 66 has these words: 'Even marching through the flood on foot, there we in him were glad.' David wrote that psalm many years after the 'flood,' the deliverance from the Red Sea. But you see, David was identifying himself with the works of God in days past. He is part of the church and, you see, what happened to one part of the church is a matter of praise in the whole of the church. When we come to glory and look back, we shall not only praise God for what happened in our individual lives and in the life of our congregation and in the life of our denomination, but we are going to praise God for what he did for his people in all ages. That is going to be our praise and worship and thanksgiving in heaven. We are identifying ourselves with the church of God in all ages.

Some people give you the impression that the church only began properly perhaps even this century. Quite extensive denominations have come into the fore only this century and you almost think the church has begun then! But the church goes back through the Reformation to the people of God in all generations and centuries—back down to the time of the apostles and then right down through the Old Testament. All their history is for our study, for our consideration, that we may trace the works of God, that we may indeed acknowledge the hand of God in them. They are to become matters for praise in our lives. We have to read history. You might say, 'We don't have much history of the church here in Singapore.' But you have so many books where you can read about the history of the church in the Reformation, in Europe and the United Kingdom and America. That is part of your heritage too, because the church is one throughout the whole world. Let us do these things and let us consider these things and there will be matters for praise and thanksgiving to God as we acknowledge the glory of God in them.

We can see that it is a great encouragement to us as we look back on providences in our lives, that they give us confidence for the future. Sometimes we come up against difficulties and we say, 'This is something new.' But really it is not new. There is nothing new under the sun. The church has been here before. We have been here before, and we can look back on deliverances of a similar kind in the church in the past.

Remember how David put it when he was facing Goliath. 'The God who delivered me out of the paw of the lion and out of the paw of the bear will deliver from this Philistine.' He was looking back on his life and he was looking at providence and what happened to him in a previous situation. Well, providence intervened. Providence helped him out before. Is providence not going to help him out again? Providence is not going to let him down because providence is working for him, for all the children of God, for all the church of God.

This is our confidence today—that the God who delivered the church at the Reformation, and at other times when the church seemed so low, is the God who will yet deliver us. He has delivered us from so great a death and he will yet deliver us! We get ammunition for the fight of faith we are involved in today. We get ammunition from our contemplation and our meditation and observation of what God has done in our lives in the past and what God has done in the life of his church and his people in days gone by.

~ 4 ~

The Design of Providence

Blessed be the God and Father of our Lord Jesus Christ, which according to his abundant mercy hath begotten us again unto a lively hope ... 6Wherein ye greatly rejoice, though now for a season, if need be, ye are in heaviness through manifold temptations: 7that the trial of your faith, being much more precious than of gold that perisheth, though it be tried with fire, might be found unto praise and honour and glory at the appearing of Jesus Christ ...   1 Peter 1:3-9

In this final talk we are going to speak about the great design of God's providence. In Romans 8 we have something of the assurance that ought to be the portion of the Christian. The Christian is a person who has great privileges and great blessings, but nevertheless along with these blessings and privileges there is to be suffering. 'If children, then heirs; heirs of God and joint heirs with Christ; if so be that we suffer with him, that we may be also glorified together' (Romans 8:17). If you are a Christian you are sure to suffer. There is no way that we shall escape suffering if we are Christians. It is part of our lot and part of our portion in this present life. It is part of being united to Christ. It is part of being a joint-heir with Christ. 'If so be that we suffer with him, that we may also be glorified together.' We are not going to be glorified unless we partake of suffering in this present life.

There are of course consolations which Paul puts before us with regard to that suffering. For one thing, there is a hope set before us. We have a hope. We are saved by hope. We are saved by the expectation that things are ultimately going to be transformed and changed—not only our souls and bodies but the whole creation. We are saved by hope, in the expectation of what is to come.

As part of our consolation we also have the Spirit's help. The Spirit helps our infirmities when we know not what to pray for as we ought. The Spirit himself maketh intercession for us with groanings which cannot be uttered.

A third consolation that Paul gives to the suffering Christian is this. 'We know that all things work together for good to them that love God, to them who are the called according to his purpose.' Then he goes on to that magnificent passage that we have in the rest of Romans 8: 'For whom he did foreknow he also did predestinate to be conformed to the image of his Son, that he might be the firstborn amongst many brethren.'

Like a pastor, Paul is dealing with a very practical situation. These Christians are suffering all kinds of persecution and trial under the Roman Empire. Paul has in mind the questions that would be raised in their minds, and the difficulties that present themselves to them. So he begins to ask questions. 'What shall we then say to these things? Who shall lay anything to the charge of God's elect? Who is he that condemneth? Who shall separate us from the love of God which is in Christ Jesus?' Paul is raising these matters because he knows they are questions that were in the minds of those to whom he is writing.

He is also giving the answers. All things are going to work together for good—and are working together for good—to those who love God, to those who are the called according to his purpose. These (and only these) are the people who have all things working together for good. They are the same people who are predestinated to be conformed to the image of his Son. These are the people for whom all things are working together for good. They are also a people, we are told, for whom he did not spare his Son, but delivered him up for us all. If he did that, how shall he not with him also freely give us all things? Besides that, says Paul, this Christ who saves us is a Christ who has been raised to the right hand of God, and who lives to make intercession for us. Who can separate us from the love of God which is in Christ Jesus our Lord? So all these things are the things that are in our favour, and pointing to the fact that God is for us.

The person for whom providence is working to a great end and purpose—the person in whose life providence is directive and purposive—is the child of God. This is the secret, you might say, that unlocks all the mysteries of life. That is what makes all the difference in our Christian experience—that we know why this is happening, that a sovereign God is causing these things to happen.

If there is any doubt as to whether God is sovereign, and loves us supremely, and has loved us with an everlasting love, and if there is any doubt that Satan may have any power outwith the control of God, what hope is there for the Christian? But if we know that God is all-powerful and all good, and has a purpose of grace for us, and is able to fulfil that purpose of grace, what a difference it makes in our life! To know that God's designs for us are all for our spiritual and eternal good! Everything is working for our spiritual and eternal good.

This is true of the individual, and those to whom Paul is writing, but it is also true of the church. The things that are true of the Christian in general are true of every individual Christian, and therefore are true of the church as a whole. God is making everything to work for good for the church, and he is making it to work together for good for the entire body of Christ. The ultimate end of that of course is the glory of his own name.

So the design of providence is to bring glory to God and to bring salvation and blessing to the souls of God's people.

1. The design of providence to bring glory to God

Firstly and briefly, how is glory brought to God in providence?

a. Providence is bringing about a glorious redemption

First of all, providence brings glory to God because in the end of all that God is doing there is going to be a restored Eden. There will be a new heavens and a new earth, in which will dwell righteousness. The first creation was spoilt by the fall of man, by the entrance of sin into the world, but God's purpose is not going to be frustrated. There is going to be a better creation, a new creation, a more glorious creation, a new community. As we said earlier, providence encompasses the whole of redemption.

So it is providence that is bringing about redemption, and the end of redemption is to have things better than they were even at the beginning. God is not going to lose out in any way by what has happened. Instead there is going to be a far greater and more glorious new creation, into which sin and death will never enter. There we will enjoy eternal life and blessedness, and never again will we be touched by the things that trouble us now in this creation, such as sin and sorrow and death. There will be no more heartache, no more tears, no more sea, nothing that divides in that eternal kingdom.

b. Providence is making known glorious things about God

The second way in which providence is working for the glory of God is that God's nature and character will have been made known in a way that would not have been made known but for redemption from the Fall.

This is a great mystery. We almost feel it is difficult to say it, but God is going to get more glory ascribed to his name through redemption from the Fall than if there had just been a creation in which no sin had entered. The creation reveals the almighty power of God, the wisdom of God and so on, but providence and redemption reveal the love of God, the goodness of God, the mercy of God, the righteousness of God. All these attributes are as it were made more glorious—not that glory can be added to God, but he is made more glorious in the eyes of his creation than if these things had not happened. 'In that salvation wrought by thee his glory is made great.' There is a greatness ascribed to God for what he has accomplished in his providence.

c. Providence gives the saints material for praise in heaven

Then thirdly, providence is working for the glory of God in the manner in which it is brought about. This will be the subject of the praise of heaven. The saints are depicted for us in the Book of Revelation, where the sea of glass is symbolic of the purity of the new heavens and the new earth. What is going to be true of the people in that place? They are going to sing the new song, the song of Moses and the Lamb. The new song is, 'Thou hast redeemed us out of every kindred, tongue and people and nation.' We look back on what has happened to us in time and what has happened to us on this earth, and that will be the subject of the praises of heaven.

Of course these praises will make mention of the glory of God in his creation. Revelation 4 is very clear that the song and the praise of those around the throne is concentrated on God as the Creator. But then you move into Revelation 5 and you have the picture of the Lamb in the midst of the throne. That is the picture of redemption. There you have this song that the redeemed sing, and it is all about what he has accomplished for them. That will be the subject of the praise of heaven.

d. Providence puts God's marvellous care of his people on display

There is one other thing that we could think about with regard to providence working for the glory of God. That is the picture we have in Ephesians 3, where Paul speaks about preaching among the Gentiles the unsearchable riches of Christ, 'to make all men see what is the fellowship of the mystery, which from the beginning of the world has been hid in God, who created all things by Jesus Christ: to the intent that now unto the principalities and powers in heavenly places might be known by the church the manifold wisdom of God.'

Remember when we were talking about Job, we said that God was putting Job on display to Satan and to the powers of darkness. 'Here is a trophy of my grace,' God was saying in effect. 'I am proud' (speaking reverently) 'of this man. He serves me because he loves me, not for what he can get out of me. You, Satan try and test him.' When Satan tries and tests him, Job maintains his integrity. So Job is a jewel (as it were) for God.

One day, says Paul, the whole church is going to be like that, the whole body of Christ. 'To the intent that now unto the principalities and powers in heavenly places might be known by the church the manifold wisdom of God.' Through the church it is going to shine so brightly as a jewel that the whole world will look at it and say, 'What a marvellous work of God!' This is something that is in keeping with what God is like. He has put this jewel on display and through this jewel, his church, polished and perfect, there is going to be a display to the whole created order—principalities and powers in heavenly places.

So the design of providence is to bring the greater glory to God.

2. The design of providence in the life of the Christian

Secondly and mainly, I want to think of five things that the design of providence has in the life of the Christian.

a. To make Christ more precious to us

The first is this, and perhaps it might surprise us to think of it. It is to make Christ more precious to us. John Flavel says that 'the due observance of providence will endear Jesus Christ every day more and more to our souls.' Why is this?

For one thing, all the mercies which providence conveys to the child of God are purchased for us by the blood of Christ. It is through him that all the streams of mercy flow to us. All the streams of providence come through the Lord Jesus Christ. Paul says, 'All things are yours.' How can all things be yours? Well, because you are Christ's and Christ is God's. We have no other title to any thing but our being in Christ. That gives us the title to everything we have—and a rightful title. The world does not have a rightful title. Everything that comes to us is the purchase of his precious blood.

Secondly, the sanctification of all our mercies is in union with the Lord Jesus Christ. The spiritual and temporal mercies that we enjoy in the providence of God were forfeited by our sin, but they are restored to us in Christ. He that spared not his own Son, but gave him up for us all, how shall he not with him freely give us all things? All things necessary for time and for eternity are ours in Christ. All things pertaining to godliness are ours in Christ. Things without Christ are worthless, but the smallest portion that we may have in this life with Christ is true blessedness. They are all blessed to our sanctification through Christ.

Thirdly, the continuance of all our mercies and comforts, outward as well as inward, is the fruit of the intercession of Christ in heaven. Paul is saying here in chapter 8 of Romans, 'He is at the right hand of God.' That is what makes all the difference. Who shall separate us from the love of Christ? Shall anything in this world? Shall tribulation? Or distress? Neither death, nor life, nor angels, nor principalities, nor powers, nor things present, nor things to come, nor height, nor depth, nor any other creature, shall be able to separate us from the love of God, which is in Christ Jesus our Lord. We are united to him who is now upon the throne of the universe, who has now got all power in heaven and earth. Everything is under his control, and the saints can be deprived of nothing that is for their good and for the glory of God.

b. To make us recognise that God is God

Secondly, the design of providence is to make us recognise that God is God. To discover, or reveal, to us who God really is.

The Mystery of Providence by John Flavel is based on Psalm 57:3: 'I will cry unto the Most High God, who is able to perform all things for me.' Flavel says a lot about the Most High God. The providences of God bring us to recognise that he is the God Most High. As Ralph Erskine said, 'Dark providences in the hand of God are in order for us to discover himself in a way suitable to himself and his glory.'[39] They show that his thoughts are not our thoughts and his ways are not our ways. They show that God is far above man, that God is the God who is transcendent, the God who is glorious.

A.W. Tozer said some 50 years ago, 'The Christian conception of God current in these middle years of the 20th century is so decadent as to be utterly beneath the dignity of the Most High God.'[40] As the gospel declines in any land or within the professing church, the great tendency is to bring God down to the size of man. It has happened in the world before.

---

[39] Paraphrased from: Erskine, R. (1737) *Dark Providences clear'd in due Time*. David Duncan, Edinburgh. p.20.
[40] Tozer, A.W. (1961) *The Knowledge of the Holy*. Harper & Row, New York: USA. p.10.

Luther said to Erasmus, 'Your thoughts of God are too human.' Very often that is the way we find ourselves, thinking of God in human terms. We might say to the evangelical church of our day, 'Your God is too small.' We have reduced him in size, in our minds and in our attitudes and in our outlooks. Lord Macaulay, a writer in England many years ago, was not a Christian, but he gave this testimony to the Puritans, that they were,

> men whose minds had derived a peculiar character from the daily contemplation of superior beings and eternal interests. Not content with acknowledging, in general terms, an overruling providence, they habitually ascribed every event to the will of the Great Being for whose power nothing was too vast, for whose inspection nothing was too minute.[41]

We have a lot to learn from the Puritans. The consideration of God as the God Most High, the supreme Lord, was the foundation of their faith and of their religion. That produced godliness.

---

[41] Macaulay, T. B. (1868) *An Essay on the Life and Works of John Milton.* Alfred Thomas Croker, London. pp.57-58.

We may have many good things in the church today, but I think what we lack above everything else is godliness. True godliness. True godliness is being answerable to the God Most High. The Puritan believer walked humbly with God, each day striving to preserve his soul in a holy frame to which grace had first reduced it. It was not enough for him to have a conversion experience. In conversion, by God's grace a sinner is humbled before God—he recognises the true God and he believes in the Lord Jesus Christ. But the Puritan believer practised a daily walk with God. He humbled himself before God in all his providential dealings with him. He was given to self-examination. He kept a diary or a journal. There was much to consider and many things to praise God for. He had a rich experience.

That is what we need so much—a rich experience. If we are not looking at the being and glory and character of God, if we are not contemplating his works, if we are not looking at his dealings with us, then we are impoverished and we become stunted in our growth. The Puritans had the advantage over us in that they had this daily contemplation of the

Most High God, this daily walk with God, and this thoughtful observance of God's providence. So there was a richness in their Christian experience, coming from reflection and meditation. We need to get back to that richness.

We know the pressures that people are under, especially in your situation. We recognise that there is so little time to give to these things. But we must take as much time as is possible for us to walk with God and to meditate on God and reflect on God. There is so much subjectivism in the church today. Our praying is focused so much on our own feelings and our own needs. We also need the objective note—to focus on God and his works. As we have said, the Puritans looked first to God and his glory and his kingdom. How that order must always be kept in our approaches to God, when we come to God in prayer! God's glory first.

The Puritans found a lot of the solutions to the problems of life in and through their waiting upon God. In the trials and tribulations of the Christian in the present day, people are looking for a trouble-free Christianity. They want to be rid of trouble.

Very often they are looking for a solution in psychology and counselling. The average Christian bookshop in the Western world is full of 'how to' books. There is a whole range of books covering how to do this and how to do that in answer to the problems of life. By contrast, the Puritans got their answers in the way that their pastors and preachers taught the whole counsel of God and applied the principles of Scripture to the people. The only true answers we will ever get are the answers that come from the Word of God and from the faith we have in the Word of God. The whole counsel of God contains all things necessary for our salvation—not only for salvation in the narrow sense of conversion, but for all that we need in this present life. It contains not only what is necessary for the being of the church but for the wellbeing of the church. It brings us to the godliness that is the reaction to God and his glory, and godliness is the great priority.

God will have a people who are godly. He uses his providences to make us recognise that he is God Most High, that he is a God who seeks his own glory, and his creatures' blessedness is also in seeking that glory. What is man's chief end? That is the first question in our Westminster Shorter Catechism. 'Man's chief end is to glorify God, and to enjoy him for ever.' People today want the joy but they do not want the duty. Where are you going to find enjoyment? Where are you going to find blessedness? Not by seeking blessedness, not by seeking enjoyment! The scriptural order is to glorify God, and then you will find true blessedness. When God Most High is acknowledged for who he is, there will be godliness in life and conversation. Providence is seeking to bring us to that. That is one of the great designs of providence.

c. To make us trusting and contented in our lives

A third design of providence is to make us trustful and contented in our lives. Who of all people ought to be more trusting and contented in this life than the Christian? Christians can rest confident in the care of providence to supply all our needs.

Surely that is what the Lord Jesus Christ was teaching his disciples in the Sermon on the Mount, in that famous passage where he speaks about the things that are around us. 'Wherefore I say unto you, take no thought for your life, what ye shall eat, or what ye shall drink, nor yet for your body, what ye shall put on. Is not the life more than meat, and the body than raiment? Behold the fowls of the air, for they sow not, neither do they reap, nor gather into barns, yet your heavenly Father feedeth them. Are ye not much better than they?' (Matthew 6:25) He is arguing from the lesser to the greater. Here is the God of providence and he is feeding the whole of his creation. He is feeding the birds and the animals, he is providing for them, they wait upon him and they get their meat in due season.

Now that is a lesson for us. God is concerned for sparrows. Are you not much better than they? If God our heavenly Father provides for these creatures that do not have souls like we have, that are not made in the image and likeness of God, is it not so that he will care far much more for us? Are ye not much better than they?

Also Jesus takes a lesson from the grass of the field. 'If God so clothe the grass of the field, which today is, and tomorrow is cast into the oven, shall he not much more clothe you, O ye of little faith?' You are worried about your food, about what you are going to eat and drink. Well, think of the birds and the beasts who are being fed. You are worried about how you are going to be clothed, how you are going to survive, how you are going to have enough of the good things of this life. Well, consider the grass of the field. It is there for a day and it is gone. But you are going to exist for ever. You have a never dying soul. You are made in the image of God. O ye of little faith, your heavenly Father knows!

You see, of all people, the child of God should be trustful in his heavenly Father. 'My God,' says Paul, 'shall supply all your needs out of the riches of his glory in Christ Jesus.' 'His mercies are new every morning, great is his faithfulness.' What matters to the Christian more than anything else is surely that he has the favour of God in all these things. In Psalm 4, a psalm of great comfort for the child of God, the psalmist comments, 'There are many people who say, Who will show us any good?' That is the attitude of the world. 'Who will show us any good? What good can we get?' Well, this is the good. 'Lord, lift thou up the light of thy countenance upon us! Thou hast put gladness in my heart, more than in the time that their corn and their wine increased. I will both lay me down in peace, and sleep, for thou, Lord, only makest me dwell in safety.'

The world out there have their plenty—their corn and their wine increase—but they do not have happiness. They do not have joy. 'Thou hast put more gladness in my heart than in the time that their corn and their wine increased.' How? He had the light of God's countenance. Because he had God's favour he can lie down in peace, 'for thou, Lord, only makest me to dwell in safety.' Similarly Psalm 37:16 says, 'A little that a righteous man hath is better than the riches of many wicked.' If you have God and God's favour with your little, then you have enough to sustain you through this present life. Providence is the care God takes of his people as their heavenly Father.

Of course, providence will not supply all our wishes. Therefore we are to submit to whatever providences God sends upon us. God sometimes sends wants upon his people. He sometimes leaves them in a situation where they are in need. What are they to do? Well, in that situation they are to cry to him. There are so many instances of that in the psalms. He brings us into a position where we live in constant dependence upon him. That is why the prayer is, 'Give us this day our daily bread.' We are not promised anything for tomorrow or for the next day. We are promised for this day, supply for our needs. And it is this way that God keeps us in dependence upon himself. We are to live in dependence on God.

And as we receive from his hand every providence that comes to us, it has the love of God written on it. That is the joy that the Christian has. He is in desperate need and he prays and he submits to the will of God and in due time God answers. But it is not just God giving him something as a king would bestow a gift on poor people. The providence comes with the love of God written all over it. That is what makes it so precious and such a joy to the Christian. It brings the Christian to a state of contentment.

Paul says, writing to the Philippians, 'I am very glad for the gift you sent to me.' They were taking great care and attention of the apostle in his need, and they sent him a gift. 'Your care of me has flourished.

I am very pleased about that motivation you have had. But,' he says, 'not that I speak in respect of want, because I have learned in whatsoever state I am, therewith to be content.' That is the great thing.

The Puritans used to speak about us being emptied from vessel to vessel. God would change our circumstances. He would change them suddenly, perhaps, and change from one condition to another, but the whole purpose of it is to bring us at the end to a contentment with what we have. There is a verse in the Psalms which says, 'Because they have no changes, therefore they fear not God' (Psalm 55:19). On the whole the course of the wicked is a smooth way. They get on in the world and nothing upsets them much. But God will not permit his people to settle down in this world, and so he sends changes into their condition. They know poverty, they know sickness, they know difficulties and trials, and there are changes. What do the changes bring? They bring the fear of God. It brings contentment with God.

d. To prove that our Christianity is genuine

Fourthly, God's design in providence is to prove that our Christianity is genuine, and to bring us to bear fruit for his glory and for greater usefulness in our lives in this world.

That is what Peter tells us. '… the trial of your faith, being much more precious than of gold that perisheth, though it be tried with fire, might be found unto praise and honour and glory at the appearing of Jesus Christ.' In providence God tries the faith of his people through affliction and through trial.

As I have mentioned, Thomas Boston, the great Scottish preacher, wrote a book called *The Crook in the Lot*. Boston says that the crook in the lot is 'the great engine of providence for making men appear in their true colours.'[42] The crook in the lot is some trial or difficulty, some thing that happens, a sickness in your life, something in your family that you have to bear with. What does it do? It makes us

---

[42] Boston, T. (1863) *The Crook in the Lot*. Porteous and Hislop, Glasgow. p.35.

appear in our true colours. Along somewhat similar lines, C. S. Lewis, a popular writer in England, said that afflictions are blockades in the road to hell. People would be going to hell, as it were, but God puts a blockade in the way. Some great trial will sometimes turn people off the road to hell and turn them to God. Then Andrew Fuller says that afflictions refine some and consume others. It is like the sun, which melts the ice and hardens the clay. A fiery trial hardens some people and turns them against God, and melts other people (the true children of God) and draws them closer to God.

That is what Peter is saying. It is the trial that determines the authenticity of your faith. 'That the trial of your faith, being much more precious than gold that perisheth, though it be tried with fire, might be found unto praise and honour and glory at the appearing of Jesus Christ.' The trial of fire is going to test you, whether you are a true Christian or not. According to the Westminster Confession of Faith,

> The most wise, righteous and gracious God doth oftentimes leave for a season his own children to manifold temptations, and the corruption of their

own hearts, to chastise them for their former sins,
or to discover unto them the hidden strength of
corruption and deceitfulness of their hearts, that
they may be humbled; and to raise them to a more
close and constant dependence for their support
upon himself, and to make them more watchful
against all future occasions of sin, and for sundry
other just and holy ends. (WCF 5.5)

What a very practical and pastoral approach to the
doctrine of providence! The Confession sets forth
this great purpose that God has, in not only trying
us to show that we are true Christians, but also to
bring us to know him better and to depend more
upon his grace. Why did Paul have the thorn in the
flesh? No one can ultimately determine what was
Paul's thorn in the flesh. Volumes have been written
upon it. But all we know is that it was something
very difficult, something that was a great and
severe trial. How did Paul look upon it? Well, he
saw it as God's means to keep him humble, and to
keep him useful in the cause of Christ. 'My grace is
sufficient for you: my strength is made perfect in
weakness.' 'I will glory in infirmities,' he says, 'that
the power of Christ may rest upon me.' God had a
purpose in it, and it was to make Paul more useful,

and to keep him humble, and to keep him usable in the hand of God.

Martin Luther said, 'I never knew the meaning of God's Word till I came into affliction.'[43] There is a sense in which affliction brings us to know things that we would not know otherwise. 'Before I was afflicted,' says the psalmist, 'I went astray, but now I keep thy word.' God's providence in affliction was a means by which the psalmist was kept from straying, and brought back to the Word of God.

I think the passage in John 15 about the vinedresser and the vine and the branches is one which has great significance as far as our Christian lives are concerned. The Father is the vinedresser, Christ is the vine, and we are the branches. What does the Father do? He is pruning the branches. The knife may be sometimes very sharp, and as the hand of the vinedresser reaches you, you will feel it. It will hurt you, just like Joseph felt it. But what is he doing in it all? He is doing it in order to produce fruitfulness in your life. There is no fruitfulness

---

[43] *The Christian Miscelleny and Family Visitor* (1848) John Mason, London. Vol. 3, January issue, p.10.

except there is pruning. That is true of most fruit trees. They need to be pruned if they are to bring forth fruit. So in the Christian life we need to be pruned. We need to feel the sharp knife of God in our lives if there is going to be fruitfulness.

Charles Haddon Spurgeon says that God brings his best soldiers out of the highlands of affliction. How that was true in his own experience! Today part of the great concern of certain movements in the church is that we should be delivered from sickness. What a different view we have in the life of C.H. Spurgeon! This is what was said in his autobiography *The Full Harvest*:

> Undergirding all Spurgeon's experience in suffering was his conviction that his ill-health was God's gift. He gained from illness a wealth of knowledge and sympathy which he could not have gained elsewhere. In the realms of sorrow he was blessed. With his own experience in view he warned his students near the end of his life against making a mistake over what is a blessing: 'In the matter of faith-healing health is set before us as if it were the great thing to be desired above all other things. Is it so? I venture to say that the greatest

earthly blessing that God can give to any of us is health, *with the exception of sickness*. Sickness has frequently been of more use to the saints of God than health has. ... A sick wife, a newly-dug grave, poverty, slander, sinking of spirit, might teach us lessons nowhere else to be learned so well. Trials drive us to the realities of religion.'[44]

Spurgeon's son, Charles Spurgeon, Jr. said,

I know of no one who could, more sweetly than my dear father, impart comfort to bleeding hearts and sad spirits. As the crushing of the flower causes it to yield its aroma, so he, having endured in the long-continued illness of my beloved mother, and also constant pains in himself, was able to sympathise most tenderly with all sufferers.[45]

The concept of the crushing of the flower causing the sweet aroma to arise is a beautiful analogy for how God uses afflictions in the lives of his people. If you remember, I relied a great deal in the earlier lectures on what B.B. Warfield had to say about

---

[44] Spurgeon, C.H. (1973) *The Full Harvest*. Banner of Truth, Edinburgh. p.414.
[45] *Op. cit.*

providence. The interesting thing about Warfield is that when he got married, he and his wife went to Germany on their honeymoon. In Germany his wife was struck by lightning, and it left her an invalid for the rest of her life. She was confined largely to bed in the home. Here is this great preacher and great theologian pouring out all his theology, instructing his classes, writing these great volumes, and back at home he had this sore trial and affliction, nursing his invalid wife all her days.

You see, there is a connection. There was the crushing of the flower and the coming forth of fruit to the glory of God. Thomas Boston, another of my favourites, spent his life preaching in the Borders of Scotland. His wife was subject to terrible depression. She was bedridden most of their married life, their children were dying around them, and he was a busy preacher, pastor, expositor, theologian, and churchman. Boston says that the usual way of providence with him was that blessing comes through several iron gates.[46] How did he have blessing in his life? Well, the blessing came out of the trials. And like Spurgeon, Boston's writings are encompassing the globe today. They are speaking to us after three centuries. They are proclaiming the glorious God and the salvation of the Lord Jesus Christ.

e. To prepare us for glory

The fifth design of providence is to prepare us for glory. Surely that is the ultimate end. Afflictive providences drive us to God. Thomas Watson, the Puritan, who writes so well and so clearly and so attractively, says that when God lays a man on his back, then he looks up to heaven.

God may lay us low, but it is in order to make us look to heaven. He has to teach us that the greatest blessing of all is himself. He has to teach us that all we have is in him. That is the story of Psalm 73. The psalmist had such great problems with regard to the

---

[46] 'It is the usual way of providence with me, that matters of moment come through several iron gates.' Boston, T. (1988) *Memoirs*. Banner of Truth, Edinburgh. p.282.

wicked and their prosperity, but when he went into the house of God he saw things in a new perspective. When he comes to himself, and to the realisation of what his position truly is, what does he say? 'Whom have I in the heavens high, but thee, o Lord, alone? and there is none upon earth that I desire beside thee. My flesh and my heart faint and fail, but God is the strength of my heart and my portion for ever.' The psalmist is ready for heaven because he has found God as his portion.

And that is what heaven will be like. God is the all-sufficient portion of his people. If we lived in comfort and ease and had all the good things of this life, how would we be prepared for heaven? That is the wrongness of the health and wealth gospel. We are not looking for a utopia here on earth. Our utopia is in heaven. The blessedness is in heaven. As Thomas Watson says, 'The vessels of mercy are first seasoned with affliction and the wine of glory is poured in at the end of the day.'[47]

---

[47] Watson, T. (1846) *A Divine Cordial*. Religious Tract Society, London. p.31.

Conclusion

I conclude with the words of James Durham, as it sums up what I have been saying.

> When the whole contexture and web of providence about the church and every individual member withal shall be wrought out, and in its full length and breadth, spread forth in the midst of all the redeemed, perfected, glorified and triumphant, the company standing around the throne and with admiring beholding it, there will not be found one misplaced thread or any wrong set colour in it all. God's perfect work will be manifested to all at the end of the day.[48]

---

[48] Durham, J. (1761) *Christ Crucified: or, the Marrow of the Gospel in seventy two sermons on the whole fifty third chapter of Isaiah.* M'Lean and Galbraith, Glasgow. p.xii.